To the Stars by Canoe
Una Canoa a las Estrellas

By Clayton Haswell

Illustrations by Antonio Coche Mendoza   **Foreword by Dr. Francisco Estrada-Belli**

Kaqchikel Maya translation by Antonio Cuxil   **Graphic design by Robert Allen**

Second edition

©   Maya Archaeology Initiative™ 2013

www.mayaarchaeology.org
www.idigmaya.org

A note to parents

The animal characters in this book represent mythic figures in the Mayan creation myth. Itzamná, for example, is the Sun Deity. Taking the form of an iguana, Itzamná (pronounced Its-zam-nah) is the Maya god of wisdom who brought the people medicine, writing, astronomy, mathematics and the calendar. The Moon Goddess Ixchel (pronounced Ee-shell), who also features prominently in this story, represents rain, fertility, pregnancy and birth, and in a larger sense, parents' love of their children.

Yum Kax, (pronounced Yoom-cash), also known as Ixim or the Corn God, provided the Maya with sustenance. Uo (Woh) the toad is the icon of water, supporting agriculture and human life. The feathered serpent Quetzalcoatl (Ket-sal-co-ah-tul, by his Nahuatl name, Kukulcan by his Yucatec Maya name) combines a magnificent green bird, symbolizing the wind and heavens, with a snake symbolizing earth.

The story of the mythic canoe crossing the river dates to early Mayan times, as does the myth of Itzamná extracting the first human beings from a cave. The drawings of the canoe used in this book were based on carvings on a 1300 year-old bone found beneath Temple I at Tikal, Guatemala.

Examined for mythic and aesthetic rather than literal value, these forms represent heroic attributes such as overcoming obstacles and learning to survive. Maya cosmology is one of the oldest in the Americas. Because virtually all Maya writing was burned during the Spanish conquest, their mythic forms were lost to the world for centuries. Only a few codices of Mayan history, written on bark in their highly evolved language, have survived. The stories lived on in the memories of Mayan elders, who passed them on orally for generations. Only now are archaeologists beginning to understand the meaning of the ancient glyphs carved in stone on their buildings.

In addition to Spanish and English languages the text is presented in Kaqchikel, which is one of 25 or more existing Maya languages, many of which are in danger of being lost forever. According to a recent census, Kaqchikel is spoken by more than a million people. It is our pleasure to render these elements of Maya culture here in a form accessible to children throughout the world.

Francisco Estrada-Belli

Maya Archaeology Initiative™

Para los papas

Los animalitos retratados en este libro representan personajes míticos de la historia de la creación maya Clásica. Itzamná es el dios sol, en su manifestación del mundo animal como iguana. Él le da a conocer a los humanos el maíz, la medicina, y el uso de la escritura y el calendario. La diosa Ixchel es la luna, y vive en la selva. Ella representa la lluvia, la fertilidad femenina y los niños recién nacidos así como el amor materno.

Yum Kax, es conocido también con el nombre de Ixim y es el dios del maíz. El proporciona sustento a la vida humana. Uo es un sapo, y representa el agua que favorece la vida humana y de los cultivos. La serpiente emplumada, conocida con el nombre en idioma náhuatl de Quetzalcoatl o Kukulcan en idioma Maya Yucateco, es el ave quetzal de plumas resplendentes que representa el viento, el cielo y es al mismo tiempo una serpiente que surge de la tierra y del agua del inframundo.

La historia de la canoa que cruza el río es una de las más antiguas que nos han llegado de la época prehispánica, junto al mito de Itzamná extraeyendo a los primeros hombres de una cueva. La ilustración del viaje en canoa fue inspirada por una escena incisa en un hueso humano de hace 1300 años encontrado en una tumba real debajo del Templo 1 de Tikal.

Analizados desde una perspectiva estético-moral más que literal, estos episodios enfatizan atributos heroicos, la capacidad de superar obstáculos y un concepto del universo propiamente maya. La cosmovisión maya tienes sus raíces en las épocas más antiguas de America. Debido a la destrucción de los libros prehispánicos durante la época colonial, los mitos más antiguos quedaron olvidados por siglos y solamente ahora están volviendo a ser conocidos y estudiados. Solo pocos textos de escritura jeroglífica de la época prehispánica los dan a conocer. Algunas historias y personajes antiguos quedaron en la memoria de los ancianos quienes los comparten oralmente de generación en generación.

Junto al texto en español e inglés, se presenta una traducción directa al Kaqchikel, un idioma compartido por más de un millón de habitantes del altiplano de Guatemala. El Kaqchikel es uno de más de 25 idiomas mayas, algunos de los cuales están a punto de desaparecer. Es un placer para nosotros presentar estos elementos de la cultura maya aquí en una forma accesible a los niños de todo el mundo.

Francisco Estrada-Belli

Maya Archaeology Initiative™

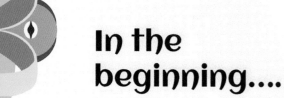

In the
beginning....

Pa ru
tikirib'äl...

En el
principio....

1

The dawn crept over a sleeping pond

A baby iguana awoke

He opened his eyes and stood on stiff legs

And sniffed at the smell of fresh smoke

Xel pe ri q'ij pa ruwi' jun alaj choy

Xk'astäj pe jun alaj inay,

Xujäq runaq' ruwäch, ruchuk'ub'an raqän

Xusäq rujub'ulik ri ya'

La madrugada llegaba a una laguna dormida

Una iguanita despertó

Abrió sus ojos y apenas se paraba en sus piernitas

Y le llegó un aroma de humo fresco

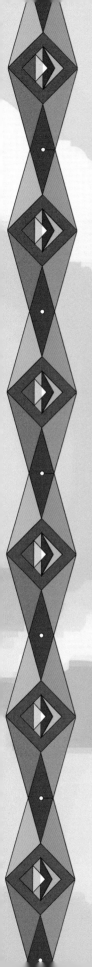

In Maya mythology, the Moon Goddess Ixchel ("Ee-shell") lived in the forest. She represented childbirth, and also the creation of medicine.

La diosa maya de la luna, Ixchel, representa la maternidad, los recién nacidos, y el amor materno.

"There's fresh roasted bug," a Goddess called out

"Help yourself to whatever you like

But don't take more than you can eat

Or you'll wind up too full to hike"

"Bicho rostizado" grito la Diosa

Sírvete lo que quieras

Pero no agarres más de lo que vas a comer

O te vas a llenar y no caminarás

K'o taq k'ilin ni'x xub'ij pe ri q'opoj Ajaw

Tachapa' ri nawajo' natïj

Xa xe mani nik'o ruwi' ri natïj

Xa man xkatikïr ta chik yab'iyin

"But where am I going?" the lizard inquired

And his spikes stuck up in the air.

"Today is the day you will hike away

And do what you once wouldn't dare"

"Po ¿akuchi' yib'e wi?, ncha' ri xpa'ch

rutzukuken rutza'n pa kaq'iq'

"Wakami ja re' xtuchäp b'ey xtuchäp b'ey xtib'e näj

Xtub'än ri majun b'ey ta rub'anon"

"Pero a donde vamos," pregunto' la lagartija

Levantando las espinas de su espalda

"Hoy es el gran día, vas a ir lejos y

Vas a hacer lo que nunca te atrevías hacer"

5

This is the Mayan glyph for Ixchel.
Este es el glifo maya para Ixchel.

Ixchel's name may have come from the Maya word for rainbow. Midwives who helped mothers give birth were known as "female lords" and were thought to have great powers.

El nombre de Ixchel pudo tener su raíz en la palabra maya para arcoíris. Las parteras eran conocidas como 'señoras' y se les atribuían poderes especiales.

"But where am I going," he asked again

A response came from high in the trees

"It's time for mankind to come to the world

Your task is to help set them free"

"Toq xkab'e ninwajo' chi nawetamaj el

Chi ri winaqi' e k'o chuwäch ri ruwach'ulew

Richin chi yeb'e xa b'akuchi'

K'atzinel chi niya' q'ij chi ke"

"A donde voy" preguntó otra vez

La respuesta vino desde lo alto en los arboles

"Es tiempo que la humanidad venga a este mundo

Y tu los vas a liberar"

6

The bugs were so crunchy he had to chew hard

It was almost like eating wet sand

"If that's what you say I'll put fear away

And do what the fates have planned"

Ri taq ni'x kan e simïl k'o chi köw yenmätz'

Kan achi'el ri ch'eqël sanayi' ketij

"Xapon k'a ri q'ij xapon k'a ri ramaj

K'o chi ninb'än achike nub'ij ri ruwa nuq'ij"

Los bichos eran tan duros le dolían sus muelas

Era como mascar arena humeda

"Si dices así voy a apartar el miedo

Y voy a hacer lo que está en mi destino"

In Maya mythology, the first living thing on Earth was an iguana known as Itzamna, and this is how they wrote his name.

En la mitología maya, el primer ser viviente fue una iguana y su nombre era Itzamná. Así se escribía su nombre.

The Moon Goddess hugged him in spite of his scales

She felt the iguana quiver

"You're on your way to the Sacred Cave

Far across the raging blue river"

Ri qati't ik' xuq'etej ri alaj inay stape' k'ix rij

Rija' xuna' chi ri alaj inay nitikïr chik nib'e ruyonil

"Rat yakowin yab'e ayonil, tachajij awi'

Nak'owisaj apo ri nïm raqän ya'"

La Diosa de la Luna lo abrazó a pesar de sus escamas

Sintió la iguana temblar

"Vete y cuídate mucho

Vete hasta la cueva sagrada

Hasta allá por el río de aguas azules"

"I can't tell you more, and
you must get moving"

She said with a nod of
her head

"Just cross the river and
head for the trees

"Now go," and her arms
were outspread

"No te puedo decir más, y
tienes que ir"

Dijo mirando hacia allá

"Cruza el río y vete hacia
los arboles"

"Anda" y abrió sus brazos.

"Majun chik xub'ij, xuchäp el
b'ey"

Majun achike chuwäch, xusiloj
rujolom

"Xa xe ok yatik'o pa ruwi' ri
nïm raqän ya' chuqa' ri nima'q
taq he'"

"Xurïk' ri ruq'a'," k'a ri' xb'e

●●●● 9

"You must be joking," Itzamná responded

"I don't even know how to swim"

But the Goddess was strong and she helped him take heart

And he knew that her faith was in him

"Rat xa yaq'olon, "xub'ij ri Itzamna

Rïn man yikowin ta yimuxan"

Po ri q'opoj Ajaw k'o ruchuq'a' xuto' richin xb'e'

Retaman chi nitikïr nub'än ruma ri xuto'

"Debes estar bromeando", contestó Itzamná

"Yo no puedo ni nadar"

Pero la Diosa fue firme y lo ayudó a tener valor

Itzamná sabía que ella confiaba en él

"Encontraras una canoa y un mono allá

Y dos viejitos que saben remar

Te llevaran sin perderse

Ahora vete nomás"

"You'll find a canoe and a monkey too

And two old guys that know how to paddle

They'll take you across without any loss

Now it's time for you to skedaddle"

"Xtawïl k'a jun juku', jun k'oy chuqa' ka'i' achi'a' richin xkatik'o apo juk'an .

Rije' choj yatkik'waj

Xoqa k'a ri ramaj chi yab'e,

Kan kaxub'an k'a

Itzamná set off
in the bright
morning sun

With Uo the Toad
at his side

The jungle was
fragrant, the
wind was still

And the two
friends fell into
stride

Itzamna xuchäp
el b'ey chuwäch
rusaqil ri q'ij

Rachib'ilan el ri
ixk'ale't

Ri k'ichelaj janila
rujub'ulik, ri kaq'ïq'
nisilon pa kiwi',

Ri ka'i' kachib'il ki'
xe'uxlan kan

Itzamná salió
hacia el sol
fuerte de la
mañana

Con el sapo Uo a
su lado

La Selva olía
fragrantemente,
el aire estaba
calmado

Los dos amigos
agarraron
camino

All he could see was a path through the trees

"There must be a river somewhere"

Itzamná was lost and his confidence sagged

So he put his green nose in the air

Jun B'atz' xsik'in pe pa ruwi' ri che'

"K'o chi k'o jun raqän ya'"

Xuluxu' ruk'u'x ri Itzamna ruma xsach kan,

K'a ri' xuchikib'a' rutza'm pa kaq'ïq'

Solo se veía un caminito entre los arboloes

"Debería de haber un río por aqui"

Itzamná perdió el rumbo y su confianza

Así que levanto su nariz verde al aire

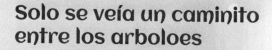

Iguanas aren't handsome, you'll have to admit	Ri taq inay man ütz ta ketzu'un, ke ri' ri kib'anikil	Las iguanas no son tan bonitas, por así decirlo
But their sense of smell is acute	Po jeb'ël ri kiseqob'al	Pero su olfato es muy agudo
Their little pink tongues can taste the air	Ri kaq' nuna' ruki'il ri kaq'ïq'	Sus lengüitas rosadas pueden saborear el aire
There's a world of ideas in their snoot	K'ïy etamab'äl k'o pa kitza'm chuqa' pa kichi'	Hay un mundo de ideas en su hocico

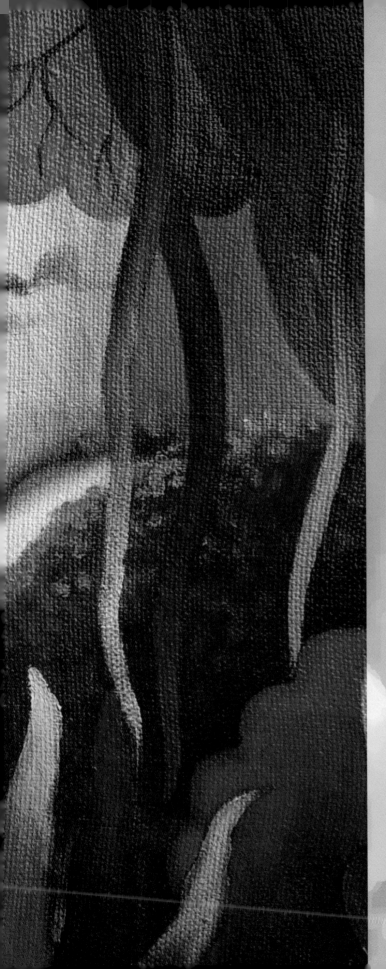

Sure as the day, I'm
happy to say

The first thing he smelled
was
the river

His ears perked up at a
trickling sound

"It's there!" And he
started to shiver

Säq Säq achi'el ri q'ij,
yikikot ruma ninb'ij apo

Ri nab'ey xinsäq ja ri
raqän ya'

Ri ruxikin xrak'axaj chi
k'o nik'ajlon

"Ja' chi la' k'o wi" k'a ri'
xb'ayb'öt pe

Seguro como el día, me
alegra decir

Lo primero que olió fue
el río

Apuntó sus orejas hacia
un ruido de burbujas

" Allá está !" Y empezó a
temblar

On the banks
of the stream
a canoe was
beached

To take them
across in style

They had no one
to paddle, no clue
where to go

Yet still he felt
himself smile

Chi ruchi' ri raqän
ya' xpa'e' jun juku'
richin xkeruk'waj,

Po majun nkixib'ij
ki' yeb'e

Pa ruwi' ri ya'
majun achike

Chi kiwäch kan
yetze'en

En la rivera había
una canoa

Para llevarlos
al otro lado con
estilo

No había
remeros, ni
motivo de ir

Pero él empezó a
sonreír

"Re' aj k'ichelaj, xub'ij apo chi re ri ixk'ale't

"Ri b'atz' chuqa' k'o chi nipe"

Po ri b'atz' xch'on pe nab'ey

Richin yojel el, k'o nik'atz'in chi qe"

"Esto va a ser divertido" Le dijo el sapo

"Y el mono vendrá con nosotros también"

Pero el mono dijo sin esperar

"Para lograrlo tenemos que ser más"

"This ought to be wild," he said to the toad

"And the monkey needs to come too"

The monkey responded before he was asked,

"To succeed we will need quite a few"

The corn god Yum Kax represented sustenance and life to the Maya.

El dios del maíz, Yum Kax, representa el sustento de la vida para los mayas. Le dio a conocer a los mayas como cultivar su comida.

"A quetzal is needed," the monkey continued

"To hold up the sky at night

And the Corn God too should join our canoe

For there might not be food in sight"

"Nos falta un quetzal", continuó el mono

Para cargar el cielo de noche

E Ixim debería de estar en la canoa también

Por si no falte comida

"k'atz'inel jun maq'uq' " xub'ij pe ri b'atz'

"Richin rutemexik ri kaj tokaq'a'

Ri rajawal ri ixim k'o chi nipe pa qajuku'

Rik'in jub'a majun ta qaq'utu'n"

Yum Kax taught the Maya how to grow food for themselves.

Yum Kax enseñó a los Mayas a cultivar el maíz para alimentarse

22

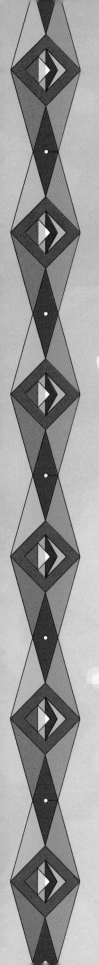

One by one they climbed aboard

And set out to cross the waves

The wind came rushing, the canoe was bounced

They must find their way to the cave

Chi jujun chi jujun xejote' el
pa juku'

Xeb'e k'a pa ruwi' ri ya'

Xpe ruchuq'a' ri kaq'ïq' k'a
ri' ri juku' xusäch rub'ey

K'o chi nikïl chik el kib'ey
chi rukanoxik ri ulew

ruma majun ta kiway.

Uno por uno subieron
a bordo

Y salieron entre las
olas

El viento dio un soplón
y la canoa brincó

Mientras buscaban la
entrada a la cueva

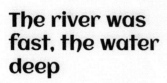

The river was
fast, the water
deep

Itzamná was
scared to death.

But with friends
all around he
kept his fear
down

Closed his eyes
and held his
breath

Ri raqän ya' xpe'
ruchuq'a' chuqa'
kan nïm rupam
ri ya'

Ri Itzamna janila
xib'iri'ïl chi re

Po kik'in ri ch'aqa'
chik rachib'il
xtane' qa.

Xutz'apij ri runaq'
ruwäch k'a ri' choj
xk'oje' qa

El río corría
fuerte y hondo

Itzamná tenía
mucho miedo

Pero con amigos
a su lado pudo
contener su
aprensión

Cerró los ojos y
la boca

25

"I think this is it," the boatmen called out,

The canoe hit its bow on the shore

"Be careful of serpents and snakes that fly

And run fast if a jaguar snores"

"Ja re' xojoqa xub'ij chi ke ri ajjuku'

Ri juku' xapon k'a chi ruchi' ri ulew

" tichajij iwi' chi kiwäch ri kumatzi', k'o kumatzi' ri yexik'an

Chuqa' xtiwak'axaj jun B'alam aninäq kixanimäj"

"Creo que aquí estamos" dijeron los remeros,

La canoa pegó en la rivera.

"Cuidado con las culebras y serpientes voladoras

Y corre si escuchas el gruñido del jaguar"

26

The six made their
way in the heat of the
day

The mountains far
off in the distance

Bugs filled the air but
no one cared

They spoke not a
single sentence

Xeb'e ri e waqi'
chuwäch ri
ruk'atanal ri q'ij,

K'a näj k'o ri k'ichelaj

xesach jub'a' ruma ri
kaq'iq'

po majun chi ke
xq'ajan majun
xech'on

Los seis avanzaron en el calor
del mediodía

Los cerros se veían a la distancia

Los bichos pululaban pero nadie
se preocupaba

No se escuchó ni una palabra

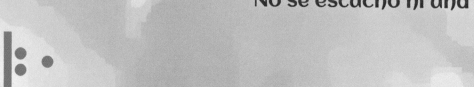

A serpent with feathers hid in a bush

And gave the hikers a fright

"Straight ahead!" said the serpent, his feathers ablaze,

"At the hummingbird take a right"

Jun kumätz k'o ruxik' xpa'e' pe pa q'ayïs

Konojel xkixib'ij ki' chuwäch,

Kan xrik'e' pe ri ruxik' ri kumätz

Akuchi' k'o jun tz'unän chi ri' yixtzale' apo ri pa ajkiq'a'

Una serpiente emplumada les paró el camino

Y los asustó

"Adelante" dijo la serpiente, con plumas de llamas

"Por allí del colibrí crucen a la derecha"

In cultures across Mesoamerica, a feathered serpent represented the link between earth and sky. Known as Quetzalcoatl (Ket-sal-co-ah-tul) and several other names, the serpent-bird also was associated with the Morning Star, Venus.

En las culturas de Mesoamerica, la serpiente emplumada representa el nexo entre la tierra y el cielo. Conocido como Quetzalcoatl y otros nombres, el ave-serpiente fue asociada con la estrella matutina, Venus.

The trail was
long, their
throats were dry

With a thirst
they could barely
endure

The rain gods
prayed and
extended their
hands

And the water
that filled them
was pure

Ri b'ey janila k'a
näj kan janila
nuchaqirisaj ri
aqul,

K'o chi yojapon

Ri rajawal ri jäb'
xeruto' jub'a'

Ri ya' xkiqüm kan
ch'ajch'öj

El camino había sido
largo, sus gargantas
estaban resecas,

Con una sed que
apenas podían
aguantar

Los dioses de la lluvias
levantaron sus remos

Y un agua purísima les
cayó encima

29

The Maya believed that water had sacred power. Rain gods known as Chaacs ("Chaacks") were said to be able to create thunder and rain.
The Chaacs also led the way to the cave where the first corn or food was found.

Los mayas creían que el agua tenía poderes sagrados. Los dioses conocidos como Chacs creaban el trueno y la lluvia. Los Chacs fueron los guías para que el hombre encontrara el primer maíz en la cueva.

The rainforest is home to thousands of birds, animals and insects that are found nowhere else on Earth. But because of logging, farming, and the growth of cities, the rainforest is disappearing quickly.

Find out what you can do to help protect it!
Visit www.idigmaya.org

La selva maya es refugio para miles de aves, animales e insectos que no existen en otras partes del planeta. Pero, debido a la tala de árboles, la cazeria, la agricultura, y el avanzar de las ciudades la selva esta desapareciendo rápidamente.

Descubre que puedes hacer para ayudar a protegerla! Visita www. idigmaya.org

After they drank
they continued to
march

Across the jungle
floor

The flowers
were blooming,
the mosquitoes
hummed

The monkeys
continued to roar

Xe'uk'ya' na, k'a
ri' xeb'e'

Chik pa k'ichelaj
yekotz'ijan ri
kotz'i'j

Yejinïn ri taq üs

Chuqa' yalan
yesik'in ri taq
b'atz'

Después de beber,
continuaron su
marcha

En todo el suelo
de la selva

Brotaban flores
y sonaban los
mosquitos

Y los monos con
su canto

At the end of a forest, beside a blue lake

They came to the end of the trail

The mountains reached skyward into the clouds

The sun bright as a quetzal's tail

Saliendo de la selva, por una laguna azul

Llegaron al fin del camino

Los cerros tocaban las nubes del cielo

El sol brillaba como la cola del quetzal

Pa ruk'isib'äl chi re ri k'ichelaj xe' ruxikin k'o jun tz'initz'öj choy

Xe'apon akuchi' kiq'ijun

Ri juyu' xeq'alajin pe chi rukojol ri sutz'

Ri q'ij xch'ich'an pe achi'el rujey jun q'uq'

"Let's climb," said Itzamná to Uo the Toad

"I'm sure the cave is this way"

But the trail disappeared and the wind whipped up

Itzamna had nothing to say

"kojote' el" xub'ij ri Itzamna chi re ri ixk'ale't

"Rïn noqa' chi nuk'u'x chi ri juyu' ke re' k'o wi"

Xb'ek'is ri b'ey chuqa ri kaq'ïq' kan niropöp

Ri Itzan majun achike xub'ij

"Subamos" le dijo Itzamná al sapo Uo

"La cueva esta por aqui"

Pero el camino se desvaneció en un soplón de aire

Iztam quedó sin palabras

The beautiful Quetzal is native to the rainforest and represented goodness and light. They were respected by the Maya, and their tail feathers were extremely valuable. Today, money in Guatemala is known as the Quetzal.

El maravilloso ave queztal es nativo de la selva y representa para los mayas la bondad y la luz. Lo respetaban mucho y las plumas de su cola resplendente eran extremadamente preciosas. Hoy, el Quetzal es la moneda nacional de Guatemala.

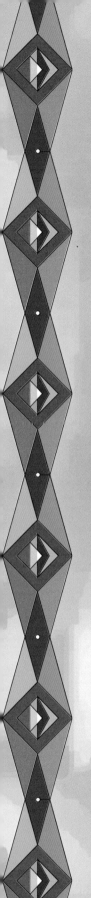

At last they came to a magical ledge

Where the earth and the sky came to meet

They looked at their feet and what did they find

But a cave of darkness quite deep

K'a ri' xeb'eqa chi ruchi' jun jul

Akuchi' Xkitzu' ri ulew chuqa' ri kaj

Rije' xkitzu' ri kaqän, ronojel ri k'o xe' kixikin

Xkïl jun nïm ruchi' juyu'

Llegaron a la orilla de un barranco mágico

Donde la tierra y el cielo se juntaban

Miraron hacia abajo entre sus pies y que vieron

Sino una cueva muy oscura y honda

Itzamna was ready, he knew what to do

Ri Itzamna xkikot ruma retaman el achike xtub'än,

Itzamná estaba listo, sabía que hacer

He reached down into the cave

Xok chupam ruchi' ri juyu'

Metió la mano dentro de la cueva

Between his fingers a human man

Toq xuna' xchap jun achi

Entre sus dedos un hombre

Kinikolo', xub'ij pe

Came out and The People were saved

Salió y eso fue la salvación de la humanidad

The toad gave him water, Yum Kax gave him corn

Itzamná set him down gently

He reached in again for the man's female friend

And wrapped her soft skin in a lily

Ri ixk'ale't xuya' ruya', Yumkax xuya' rixim

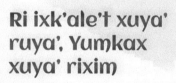

Ri Itzamna xutz'uyub'a' qa

Xoqa jun chik rachib'il ri achi

pisïl pe pa jun kotz'i'j

El sapo le dió agua, Yum Kax le dió maiz

Itzamná lo bajó suavemente

Metió la mano otra vez para buscar a su amiga

Y la envolvió en en los petalos de un lirio

Ya se acostaba el sol en el cielo rojo

Los seis sabían que había llegado la hora

Su trabajo había terminado, su misión se había cumplido

Ahora solo tenían que regresar a su tierra

Ri q'ij tajin niqa, ri kaj käq rub'anon

Ri e waqi' ketaman chi ri jeb'ël ri ruq'ijul

Xkik'ïs ri kisamaj, xoqa k'a ri ramaj

Akuchi' yetzolin chik Pa kitinamit

The sun was now setting across the red sky

The six knew the time was at hand

Their job was over, their mission complete

Time now to go back to their land

They raced down the mountain,
with time running out

They wasted no time at the cave

They reached the canoe before
the sun set

And pushed out in a headwind
and waves

Aninäq xexule' pe	De prisa bajaron corriendo entre los cerros
Man k'ïy ta ramaj xkib'än chupam ri juyu'	No perdieron más tiempo en la cueva
K'a jani' nokoq'a' pe xeb'e qa rik'in ri juku'	Alcanzaron su canoa antes de la puesta del sol
Xeb'e pa ruwi' ri choy kan janila kaq'ïq'	La empujaron contra el viento y las olas

40

The waves came
up, the canoe
was swamped

But the crew
paddled on
anyway

Their spirits are
bright, they're
alive tonight

Shining high in
the Milky Way

Xk'is ri tzijonïk,
wetaman k'a ri', rïx
xixna'ojin

Chi ri juku' majun
xapon ta chi ruchi'
ri choy.

Tokaq'a' tikirel
nitz'etetäj ri juku'

Näj k'o chuwa ri
kaj

Las olas
crecieron, la
canoa se hundía

Pero los remeros
remaron mucho

Sus almas
fuertes y claras
se ven de noche

Brillando en la
Vía Láctea del
cielo

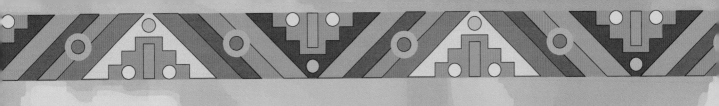

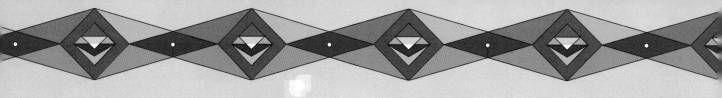

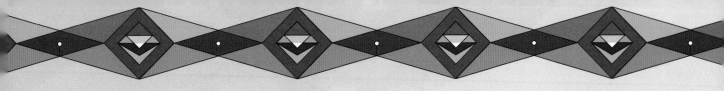

And so it
began...

K'ari x
tikir k'a ri

Y asi
empezo'...

About this book:

Clayton Haswell, the author, is chairman of the Maya Archaeology Initiative. He spent 35 years in the media industry and was a co-founder of the World Free Press Institute. He lives in Northern California.

Clayton Haswell, el autor de este libro, es director de la Maya Archaeology Initiative. Ha trabajado por 35 años en los medios de comunicación, es co-fundador de World Free Press Institute y vive en el norte de California.

Antonio Coche Mendoza, the illustrator, was born in the Tzutujil Maya village of San Juan la Laguna on Lake Atitlan. He began to draw with crayons and tempera on paper at age 7, and in 1980 began to paint in oil on canvas. He has exhibited widely both in Guatemala and in galleries outside the country, where he has gained numerous awards.

Antonio Coche Mendoza, el ilustrador, nació en San Juan La Laguna, un poblado Tzutuhil del Lago de Atitlán, Guatemala. Comenzó a dibujar con crayolas a los 7 años de edad y pinta al óleo desde 1980.

Dr. Francisco Estrada-Belli is a Guatemalan archaeologist who specializes in the beginning of Mayan history. He is president of the Maya Archaeology Initiative and teaches archaeology at Tulane University.

El Dr. Francisco Estrada-Belli es un arqueólogo guatemalteco especializado en el origines de la historia maya. Es presidente de la Maya Arqueology Initiative y docente de arqueología en la Universidad de Tulane en la ciudad de Nueva Orleans.

Antonio Cuxil, a member of the Kaqchiquel Maya community, directed the Maya artists in the creation of this book, translated the text into Mayan and consulted on mythic characters. He is a native of Chimaltengo, Guatemala and has expertise in Maya history, archaeology and epigraphy. He is fluent in Kaqchiquel, English, French, German and Spanish.

Antonio Cuxil es miembro de la comunidad Maya-Kaqchiquel en Guatelama. Ha colaboro con el artista maya en la elaboración de las ilustraciones, la traducción al kaqchiquel y consultoría sobre los personajes del libro. Nacido en Chimaltenango, Guatemala, es experto de historia, arqueología y epigrafía maya. Habla Kaqchiquel, Inglés, Francés, Alemán y Español.

Maya Archaeology Initiative™ 2013

Proceeds from this book will be used to support education programs for Maya children and traditional Maya artists. The Maya Archaeology Initiative is a non-profit 501(c)3 established to increase cultural and educational opportunities for children, protect biodiversity in the Guatemala rainforest and support the study of Maya antiquities. Contributions, which can be made on our website, are greatly appreciated.

www.mayaarchaeology.org
www.idigmaya.org

Todos los ingresos de la venta de este libro serán utilizados para financiar la educación de la niñez y las artes tradicionales mayas en Guatemala. La Maya Archaeology Initiative es una organización sin fines de lucro establecida en EEUU (501 (c)3) para promover las oportunidades de educación de la niñez, preservar la biodiversidad de la selva tropical, y la investigación de la arqueología maya en Guatemala. Visitenos en http://idigmaya.org. Gracias por su donación.

15808353R00031

Printed in Great Britain
by Amazon